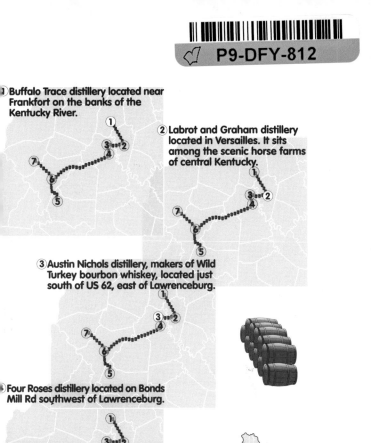

1 Buffalo Trace distillery located near Frankfort on the banks of the Kentucky River.

2 Labrot and Graham distillery located in Versailles. It sits among the scenic horse farms of central Kentucky.

3 Austin Nichols distillery, makers of Wild Turkey bourbon whiskey, located just south of US 62, east of Lawrenceburg.

4 Four Roses distillery located on Bonds Mill Rd southwest of Lawrenceburg.

THE KENTUCKY MINT JULEP

The Kentucky Mint Julep

COLONEL JOE NICKELL

The University Press of Kentucky

*Publication of this volume was made possible in part by a grant
from the National Endowment for the Humanities.*

Copyright © 2003 by The University Press of Kentucky
Scholarly publisher for the Commonwealth,
serving Bellarmine University, Berea College, Centre
College of Kentucky, Eastern Kentucky University,
The Filson Historical Society, Georgetown College,
Kentucky Historical Society, Kentucky State University,
Morehead State University, Murray State University,
Northern Kentucky University, Transylvania University,
University of Kentucky, University of Louisville,
and Western Kentucky University.

Editorial and Sales Offices: The University Press of Kentucky
663 South Limestone Street, Lexington, Kentucky 40508-4008
www.kentuckypress.com

14   13   12   11   10   6   7   8   9   10

Library of Congress Cataloging-in-Publication Data

Nickell, Joe.
  The Kentucky mint julep / Joe Nickell.
    p. cm.
  ISBN-10: 0-8131-2275-9 (cloth : alk. paper)
  1. Mint juleps—Kentucky. I. Title.
TX951.N56 2003
641.8'74—dc21

                                        2003001398

  ISBN-13: 978-0-8131-2275-5 (cloth : alk. paper)

This book is printed on acid-free recycled paper meeting
the requirements of the American National Standard
for Permanence in Paper for Printed Library Materials.

Manufactured in the United States of America.

Member of the Association of
American University Presses

CONTENTS

PREFACE

My interest in the mint julep was sparked after I left Kentucky for Buffalo in mid-1995 to become Senior Research Fellow at the Center for Inquiry. (There I currently investigate paranormal and fringe-science claims and write the "Investigative Files" column for *Skeptical Inquirer* magazine.) As a parting gift I had received from my fellow Confederation executive board members, "for service to The Historical Confederation of Kentucky," a gleaming "Kentucky's Julep Cup" (as is engraved on its underside) handcrafted by Salisbury Pewter.

For a time (I am ashamed to say) the cup languished in a cupboard, then (horrors!) served as a pen and pencil caddy atop my office desk. But as I outfitted a home bar I came to realize that I should know more about the historical concoction for which the cup was intended—especially given my background in historical research and the fact that I, like the late Harland Sanders of Kentucky Fried Chicken fame, am a Kentucky Colonel, an honor bestowed by a certificate from the governor of the commonwealth.

Bartender at the annual dinner of the The Honorable Order of Kentucky Colonels. *Kentucky Historical Society, The Kentucky Colonels Collection.*

This little book is a distillation, so to speak, of the fruits of my research—and considerable experimentation—regarding the Kentucky mint julep. I searched the archives at the University of Kentucky, collected mixed-drink guides old and new, challenged bartenders, and, of course, mixed and sipped and mixed again. I sought out whiskey collectibles and even at times maintained potted mint plants, acquiring an intimate acquaintance with *Mentha spicata.*

I had not originally intended to write a book on the subject of juleps. But a lighthearted remark over a lunch with The

University Press of Kentucky's then-director Kenneth Cherry and managing editor Angelique Galskis (a lunch sans spirits, by the way) soon had the two of them talking, as I sat momentarily ignored. "A small book," said one. "But a quality edition," replied the other. "Modestly priced," said the first, and so on.

Here, then, is the rich tradition that is the Kentucky mint julep—a bit of history and lore as well as a number of recipes, each having its own philosophical twist. Relax, read, mix, and enjoy!

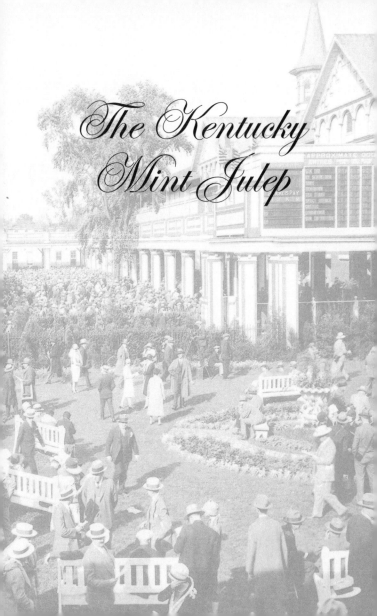

The Kentucky Mint Julep

THE KENTUCKY MINT JULEP

The mint julep is not only a Kentucky favorite or even a mere southern tradition; it is indeed an American classic that excites passion, curiosity, and more than a little enchantment. The exercise of writing about our uniquely southern spirits inspires in a writer a tendency toward reminiscence and high-flown phrases. It is held "unquestionably" to be "the most famous of the renowned classic bourbon drinks."[1]

The essential mint julep is made with bourbon and mint syrup poured over ice and garnished with a sprig of fresh mint.[2] Variations abound, some of them so far from the Kentucky julep as to be unrecognizable to traditionalists.

On the first Saturday in May, Kentucky Derby day, juleps are served at parties nationwide, yet few people know its history, and even many experienced bartenders do not know how to properly mix this celebrated drink.

THE JULEP

The use of the word *julep* dates to ancient times. The term appears to derive from the Persian *gulab*, meaning "rosewater." In Arabic the word is *julab*; in Medieval Latin *julapium*; in Spanish and Portuguese *julepe*. *Julep* is French. *The Oxford English Dictionary* records the use of the word as early as 1400 A.D. to refer to a syrup that was typically used as a vehicle for medicine. In his pioneering lexicon, *A Dictionary of the English Language* (1755), Dr. Samuel Johnson defines *julap* [*sic*] as an "extemporaneous form of medicine, made of simple and compound water sweetened, serving for a vehicle to other forms not so convenient to take alone." Long before Mary Poppins sang about a spoonful of sugar making the medicine go down, people used syrup to make bitter or otherwise disagreeable potions more palatable.

The julep as a drink was once taken as a form of cordial, a stimulating and invigorating medicine or beverage. Poet John Milton (1608–1674) described the beauty and scent of one such concoction in his poem *Comus*.

Churchill Downs clubhouse garden on Derby Day, 1927. *Photo by Caufield and Shook. Kentucky Historical Society.*

...this cordial julep here

That flames and dances in his crystal bounds,

With spirits of balm and fragrant syrups mix'd. (6, 2)

Diarist Samuel Pepys (1633–1703) evidently found julep worth some physical exertion. He wrote that on June 22, 1660, he proceeded "thence to my Lord's and had the great walk to Brigham's, who gave me a case of good julep."[3]

From its humble beginnings as a medicinal base, the julep emerged as a standard whiskey drink. The two uses, however,

Mrs. Anna Friedman, keeper of the seal
for the Honorable Order of the Kentucky Colonels.
Kentucky Historical Society,
The Kentucky Colonels Collection.

may have been similar in the beginning. One theorist suggests that "the first mint juleps could easily have been made to mask the flavor of a rough whiskey before the bourbon distillers, as we know them, had honed their craft."[4] British traveler and Virginia plantation tutor John Davis mentioned the drink in his 1803 *Travels of Four Years and a Half in the United States,* speaking of a "dram of spirituous liquor that has mint in it, taken by Virginians of a morning."[5]

THE MINT

The mint transformed the julep, according to one authority, into "our own American invention." Adding mint was a logical and successful step. "Of all the compatibles man has discovered in the world of food and drink," writes Gerald Carson, "none excels the harmony with which mint blends into a silver goblet filled with ice, a dusting of sugar and several ounces of mellow bourbon."[6]

The mint used in juleps is common English garden mint, *Mentha spicata,* or spearmint, which is also used for making candy, tea,[7] and jelly. The plant is also said to have many medicinal properties, including the ability to settle a queasy stomach, increase appetite, sweeten the breath, relieve the sting of an insect bite, and cure chapped skin. The tiny spikes of flowers are said to attract beneficial insects to gardens, and the leaves are used to repel rodents. Pliny wrote that "the smell of Mint does stir up the Minde."[8]

The single greatest debate involving the mint julep is over whether to crush the mint leaves or not. According to one writer (perhaps with hyperbole), "Duels have been fought over this question."[9] One late-nineteenth-century authority said that the matter depends on the strength of the mint, but he stipulated that the leaves should be crushed and allowed to stand before the bourbon was added.[10]

In contrast is the opinion of the author of a southern cookbook, who gives a reason for her opposition to crushing the leaves: Doing so "releases the bitter, inner juices." Therefore, this source advises readers to "bruise the mint gently with a muddler and blend the ingredients by stirring and pressing gently for several minutes."[11] The notion that the mint is "only for bouquet"[12]—as one mixologist suggests—defies tradition and logic. (I suggest yet another option; see "Colonel Nickell's Perfect Julep.")

Virginians may have indulged in a bit of mint and spirits in the morning, but more than one Kentuckian has described the inspiration found in the fragrant beds of mint clustered around clear springs of cold water. And more than one has claimed to have thought, as did former Kentucky governor Simon Bolivar Buckner, of how well the two would mix with a little sugar and a healthy helping of bourbon.[13]

THE BOURBON

Of course the main ingredient of the mint julep is whiskey, a liquor with a long and interesting history. In the latter part of the eighteenth century, those on the western frontier had difficulty bringing their crops to market and found that spirits distilled from the grain they grew were easier to ship than the grain itself. Barley and rye, the grains most often used for making whiskey, became significant cash crops, and distilling became an adjunct to farming. Alexander Hamilton, America's first secretary of the treasury, saw this large whiskey output as a source of revenue for the fledgling country. The resulting whiskey tax of 1791 was rejected by the independent-minded farmers, and in 1794 President Washington was forced to send out the militia to quash the Whiskey Rebellion.[14]

Although whiskey was originally produced from rye and barley, when corn began to be used the product became a distinctly American original. Today, according to federal law, bourbon whiskey must be made from grain consisting of at least 51 percent corn, whether it is straight or blended (made

Warehouse at the Lobrot and Graham Distillery. *Kentucky Historical Society, Wolff, Groller, Cusick, Hill Studio Negative Collection.*

from a mixture of bourbon from various distilleries). In the case of blended whiskey, the age on the label indicates the youngest liquor that was used in the mixture. Tennessee whiskey, unlike fine Kentucky bourbon, is made from a mash that contains "at least 51 percent corn *or any other grain.*"[15])

In the late eighteenth century a new type of whiskey emerged, taking its name from the area of Bourbon County created in 1786 in what was then the District of Kentucky in Virginia. According to legend, bourbon whiskey, as it came to be known, was the creation of the Reverend Elijah Craig in 1789. A Baptist minister who founded the first paper mill west of the Alleghenies,[11] Craig supposedly recycled some oak barrels by burning their interiors and later aged some whiskey in one of the charred barrels. The resulting liquor was smoother and mellower than ordinary whiskey and had a superior flavor and distinctive color. The charred-barrel process soon spread throughout the region, and the product became known as "Old Bourbon whiskey," later simply "bourbon."[16]

Skeptics, however, point out that there is little evidence for the Craig claim other than the mere assertion of historian Richard Collins long after the fact, in 1874. And Craig's distillery was not located in Bourbon County or even in the much larger Old Bourbon region but in nearby Fayette County, in an area that later became Woodford County, and today is part of Scott County.[17]

Nevertheless, someone in Kentucky began to use charred barrels, and the process resulted in "a noticeably different whiskey" by the time it reached New Orleans. Residents there wanted more of the "amber-colored whiskey from Bourbon."[18] Bourbon was thus a Kentucky creation. (Never mind that, if it was first made before statehood in 1792, the invention technically occurred in Virginia).

THE DRINK

Rye, scotch, rum, brandy, gin, even champagne, can be, and have been, combined with mint syrup to make a "mint julep."[19] Bourbon, however, "the most famous American whiskey,"[20] became forever wedded to the mint julep and sealed Kentucky's claim to the drink. As early as 1816, Kentuckians were "awarding silver julep cups as prizes at county fairs,"[21] and the rest, as they say, is history.

At Churchill Downs, site of the Kentucky Derby, the clubhouse served mint juleps at the racetrack's inception in 1875. Reportedly, mint grew conveniently out back. According to the Kentucky Derby Museum's curator, the mint julep probably did not become the Downs' signature drink until 1938, at which time management began selling the drink—in souvenir glasses—for seventy-five cents each.[22]

Julep Lore

Witticisms and tales abound regarding
the classic bourbon drink.

DICKENS AND IRVING

In 1842 at a hotel in Baltimore, Charles Dickens and Washington Irving discussed the qualities of an especially large mint julep. Dickens later wrote: "It was quite an enchanted julep and carried us among innumerable people and places that we both knew. That julep held out far into the night." Ever after that night, Dickens claimed that he never saw Irving in his mind's eye without that julep, "bending over it, with his straw, with an attempted air of gravity."[23]

ORATOR ON BOURBON

Colonel Robert G. Ingersoll (1833–1899), noted lawyer, Union Army officer, writer, agnostic, orator, and one-time member of the U.S. House of Representatives, called bourbon "liquid joy." He credited "the dreamy, tawny dusks of many perfect days" that the liquor had spent "within the happy staves of oak."[24]

A QUESTION OF TEMPERANCE

The following story was told by one-time Kentucky governor Simon Bolivar Buckner (1823–1914). At the time he was eighty-five years old and being visited by a group of Nashville newspapermen. He discussed his service as lieutenant-general in the Confederacy and related other reminiscences and stories before he suddenly broke out with a tale that revealed him as a true politician and a Kentuckian.

I must tell you an anecdote—how I won an old Prohibitionist in my canvass for the nomination for Governor. I was in Winchester, up in the bluegrass region, in the office of my friend, Capt. Lee Hathaway, a Confederate soldier. A number of gentlemen were in there on a cool autumn evening. Whilst we were there talking an old gentleman came in, a very nice-looking old fellow, an old farmer. He had on one of those long-tailed coats coming down to his heels and buttoned up to the chin. His face was clean-shaven. There wasn't a hair on it, and his appearance was that of a man whose thoughts had been of too serious a character all his life. He looked as if, had he attempted to smile, it might have cracked the surface. You have seen men of that sort. On being introduced, he said to me:

"Gen. Buckner, I haven't yet made up my mind, sir, as to whom I will support for Governor, and before I decide I wish to ask you a question, sir."

I told him I recognized his perfect right to do that.

"I wish to know, sir, your opinion of officials drinking whisky. For my part, sir, I think they ought not to drink any at all, because it might interfere with the clear exercise of their judgment."

Said I: "I recognize, sir, the propriety of your question, and I will answer it with entire frankness. I am a temperate man; was never intoxicated in my life, and never expect to be; but at the same time, sir, I live in a very remote part of this country from your beautiful bluegrass region here—down in the knobs of Green River, on the place where I was born, and which I love very much; but I am especially fond of a beautiful spring on my place," said I. "It has a large volume of water gushing out of the rocks and flowing over a number of little precipices, forming a series of beautiful cascades, until the water mingles

with that of the brook that flows at the base of the hill,"
says I. 'Around the mouth of this spring, growing in great
profusion, are immense beds of mint, its roots watered
by the cool spring, and diffusing its aroma in all the air
around; and as I sit upon the banks of that stream, lis-
tening to its murmurings over the rocks, it does seem to
me, sir, that it is clamoring for some other ingredient to
mix with them. So I keep that ingredient at my house, and
if I can induce a friend, by its intricate approaches, to
that sequestered spot, I invariably put these three ele-
ments before him, with a little sugar, and tell him to mix
them to suit himself. And I have read in books of Oriental travel where the people of the East are in the habit of
poisoning each other, it was the custom of the host to taste
his own poison first, to convince his guests that it would
not hurt them. I invariably follow that beautiful Oriental
custom."

He said: "I think that is allowable."

"We will try it," the General said, addressing his guests, and
no one protested.[25]

THE ESSENTIAL JULEP

Henry Watterson (1840–1921), noted newspaper editor, was responsible for the merger in 1868 that produced the *Louisville Courier-Journal*; he served that paper for over half a century and received a Pulitzer Prize in 1917.

A man of strong opinions, Watterson insisted that two glasses should be used for the mint julep: The bourbon should be poured into one, and the mint, sugar, and water into the other. "Then throw that out," he urged, "and drink the whiskey!"[26]

CAUSE OF WAR?

Many have had strong opinions about the mint julep. In 1936, Kentucky humorist Irvin S. Cobb (1876–1944) stated that his grandfather "always insisted that a man who would let the crushed leaves and the mangled stemlets steep in the finished decoction would put scorpions in a baby's bed." He also advanced his own theory on the reason for the War between the States. "Well, down our way we've always had a theory that the Civil War was not brought on by Secession or Slavery or the State's Rights issue," he wrote. "These matters contributed to the quarrel, but there is a deeper reason. It was brought on by some Yankee coming down south and putting nutmeg in a julep. So our folks just up and left the Union flat."[27] (See "Irvin S. Cobb's 'Original Kentucky Mint Julep.'")

VERSIFICATION

Clarence Ousley (1863–1948) waxed poetic on the marriage of bourbon and mint in his poem "When the Mint Is in the Liquor." He seems to agree with Charles Dickens that a julep can live on in a man's mind long after the drink has been consumed.

When the mint is in the liquor and
its fragrance on the glass,
It breathes a recollection that
can never, never pass.

KENTUCKY HOSPITALITY

Gene Markey, author of *The Kentucky Jug*, tells of a May morning when he heard that the commanding general of Fort Knox was entertaining some Panamanian air force officers. He invited the general and his guests for a drink. In preparation, he "set out a bottle of Bourbon with a few julep cups and sent Charles down the hill to our little spring to pick mint leaves." Little did he know that he had volunteered to slake the thirst of a small army. "When the general—a highly agreeable fellow—arrived, I was staggered to see behind him a whole phalanx of Panamanians," Markey wrote. "Twenty-three of them, their eyes feverish with thirst! All had heard of the Kentucky julep—and all wanted to try it. Including the general they were twenty-four and I raised the total to twenty-five. (In a leap year, twenty-nine.) My mind—never an I.B.M. computer—sought to grapple with the problem: twenty-five juleps at seven minutes each, not counting etc., etc...." The situation grew complicated. But Markey valued the famous Kentucky hospitality and was determined to please his guests. "I was committed. And, Kentucky hospitality being what it is, nobody may

Jno. G. Roach and Company advertisement. *The Filson Historical Society.*

have just one julep. For the next several hours I worked harder than a bartender at a Tammany picnic—while Charles, bearing baskets of mint, scurried up and down hill like a Sherpa guide." Markey's moral to this tale is that "in such moments of crisis it is well not to mention juleps, but to have on hand some bottles of 'prepared' Manhattan cocktails. (A repulsive thought, to be sure, but necessity is often the step-sister of invention.)"

Mint julep aficionados can identify with American writer Bret Harte, who wrote in 1891 of "a dusty drive with a julep at the end of it."

Recipes

TIPS FOR A PERFECT MINT JULEP

After culling suggestions from julep makers everywhere and evaluating and experimenting with various methods, I offer the following tips for creating the perfect Kentucky mint julep.

- Use only good Kentucky bourbon.
- Instead of granulated sugar, use superfine, which dissolves more readily.
- Serve the drink in a silver or pewter goblet or julep cup, which will frost much better than a glass.
- Pre-chill the cup thoroughly before mixing the julep.
- Use crushed or shaved ice, and stir rapidly to frost the cup.
- Use a short straw (if you use one at all) so that the mint's aroma can be savored as the drink is sipped.
- When serving, avoid touching the sides of the frosted cup and leaving unsightly smudges.

HISTORICAL JULEPS

———⚬⚬⚬———

According to Gerald Carson, "The mint
julep belongs to Kentucky and to
bourbon. In the Bluegrass State it is as
sacred as Derby Day or the memory of
Henry Clay." Following are some
historical recipes, including, appropri-
ately, the first one—from Clay
(1777–1852) himself.

Henry Clay's Mint Julep

This recipe is historically authoritative, from the diary of the Great Compromiser himself, Henry Clay. Following is the method for making a julep in Clay's own words.

The mint leaves, fresh and tender, should be pressed against a coin-silver goblet with the back of a silver spoon. Only bruise the leaves gently and then remove them from the goblet. Half fill with cracked ice. Mellow bourbon, aged in oaken barrels, is poured from the jigger and allowed to slide slowly through the cracked ice.

In another receptacle, granulated sugar is slowly mixed into chilled limestone water to make a silvery mixture as smooth as some rare Egyptian oil, then poured on top of the ice. While beads of moisture gather on the burnished exterior of the silver goblet, garnish the brim of the goblet with the choicest sprigs of mint.[28]

Kentucky Mint Julep (ca. 1898)

This recipe is traditional—and practical, since it utilizes mint syrup that can be prepared in advance and in quantity for visitors. "From the old receipt of Soule Smith," it appeared in *Kentucky Whiskies* in 1949. J. Soule Smith (1848–1904) was a Lexingtonian.

---

bourbon

water

sugar

fresh mint

Chill glasses until frosted. Make a simple syrup—boiling water and adding sugar until the consistency of oil. Crush or chop mint into syrup—to taste. Let cool.

Take 1 frosted glass. Add one teaspoon of mint syrup to bottom of glass and half-fill with crushed ice. Add 1 jigger of Kentucky Bourbon. Again add 1 teaspoon of mint syrup and finish filling with bourbon and ice—to taste. Top with a sprig of fresh mint and enjoy the bouquet.

Do not stir—let it stand a moment—when ready, sip it slowly. "Sip it and dream—you cannot dream amiss. Sip it and dream, it is a dream itself."

Mint Julep, "Southern Style" (1935)

This recipe follows the philosophy, occasionally expressed, that the mint is for "bouquet" only. It is from the *Old Mr. Boston DeLuxe Official Bartender's Guide*[29] (and naturally recommends the Boston distiller's own brand).

Fill silver mug or 12 oz. Tom Collins glass with finely shaved ice. Add 2 1/2 oz. Old Mr. Boston Kentucky Straight Bourbon Whiskey and stir until glass is heavily frosted. (Do not hold glass with hand while stirring.) Add 1 teaspoon powdered sugar and fill balance with water and stir. Decorate with 5 or 6 sprigs of fresh mint so that the tops are about 2 inches above rim of mug or glass. Use short straws so that it is necessary to bury nose in mint. The mint is intended for odor rather than taste.

Irvin S. Cobb's "Original Kentucky Mint Julep" (1936)

Kentucky author and humorist Irvin S. Cobb (1876–1944) offered the following formula for a traditional julep.[30]

Put 12 sprigs fresh mint in bowl, covered with powdered sugar and just enough water to dissolve the sugar, and crush with wooden pestle. Place half the crushed mint and liquid in the bottom of a crackled glass tumbler, or in sterling silver or pewter tankard. Fill glass half full of finely crushed ice. Add rest of crushed mint and fill remainder of glass with crushed ice. Pour in whisky until glass is brimming. Place in ice-box at least an hour (preferably two or three hours—if you can wait that long). Decorate with sprigs of mint covered with powdered sugar when ready to serve.

Mint Julep—"A Southern Recipe" (1940)

This recipe contrasts with the earlier "southern style" recipe in calling for bruising of the mint to release flavor. It is a traditional recipe (more so if one substitutes for the "tall glass" a more traditional container: a silver goblet, a silver or pewter julep cup, or an old-fashioned glass). It is found in *The Book of Herb Cookery*.[31]

Into each tall glass, put 2 or 3 sprigs of spearmint, 1 scant tsp. sugar, and half a jigger of cold water. Bruise the mint and stir until the sugar is dissolved. Add a jigger and a half (or more) of Bourbon whiskey, then fill the glass full of ice crushed as finely as possible. Beat with a long-handled spoon until glass is well frosted, adding more ice if necessary, and serve with a large sprig of mint in each glass.

CLASSIC JULEPS

A Bartender's Julep

1 cube sugar
sprigs of mint
crushed ice
3 oz. bourbon

The *Complete World Bartender Guide* instructs: "Dissolve the sugar with a few drops of water. Add a few sprigs of mint; fill the glass with ice and add the bourbon." Next, "Stir and add more mint (cut and bled) into the julep." Finally, "Allow to stand a few minutes before serving."[32] (No mention is made of garnishing, but it is traditional to top off a julep with one or more sprigs of the fresh mint.)

In one of three recipes for juleps in *The Bartender's Bible*[33] is a nice touch, which I italicize in the following adaptation.

---

6 sprigs of fresh mint

1 tsp. superfine sugar

crushed ice

3 oz. bourbon

In the bottom of a glass or julep cup, muddle 4 mint sprigs with a little water. Then *smear the mint around to coat the inside of the glass with the syrup* and discard the sprigs. Fill the glass nearly full with crushed ice and pour the bourbon over it. Add a short straw and the 2 remaining mint sprigs.

Kentucky Derby Mint Julep

According to the Kentucky Derby's Internet web site, "Over 80,000 mint juleps are served over the two-day period of the Kentucky Oaks and Kentucky Derby requiring 8,000 quarts of julep mix, 150 bushels of mint and 60 tons of snow ice."[34] The site also offers the following recipe.

---

2 cups sugar
2 cups water
sprigs of fresh mint
crushed ice
Kentucky bourbon
silver julep cups

To create a julep, the site instructs, "Make a simple syrup by boiling sugar and water together for five minutes. Cool and place in a covered container with six or eight sprigs of fresh mint, then refrigerate overnight. Make one julep at a time by filling a julep cup with crushed ice, adding one tablespoon mint syrup and two ounces of Kentucky bourbon. Stir rapidly with a spoon to frost the outside of the cup. Garnish with a sprig of fresh mint." There you have it, so to speak, from the horse's mouth.

Old Bardstown Mint Julep

This recipe is interesting because it dispenses with one traditional ingredient: water. It is offered by the Willett Distilling Company.[35]

Place 1 heaping teaspoon powdered sugar and 4 or 5 mint leaves in a julep cup or goblet and muddle together until the juice of the mint leaves has turned the sugar a little green. Then fill the cup with crushed ice and one 2 oz. jigger of Old Bardstown Bourbon (this suits our taste, but you may wish to add more) and stir continuously until the ice drops about an inch. Then fill your cup again with crushed ice, garnish with a sprig or two of mint and sprinkle top with powdered sugar. The julep cups should be frosted, so make them up half an hour ahead of time and place in your freezer and they will be frosted heavily.

Colonel Nickell's Perfect Julep

This, the author's own recipe, utilizes hot water, which more easily dissolves the sugar and draws the mint from the leaves, resulting in a perfect drink.

---

5 sprigs fresh mint
1 tsp. granulated sugar
2–3 tsp. hot water
crushed ice
2 oz. bourbon

In a measuring cup, place 4 mint sprigs and sugar and add hot water. Stir. Allow to steep and cool.

Meanwhile, fill a julep cup with crushed ice, add bourbon, and stir.

Returning to the mint, use a spoon to press the leaves against the side of the cup, then remove.

Pour the syrup over the bourbon and again stir until cup is frosted. Garnish with remaining mint sprig.

MODERN JULEPS

Southern Belles' Julep

Here is a light and fancy julep, created by the author.

---

5 fresh mint sprigs
powdered sugar
1 tsp. granulated sugar
3 tsp. water
crushed ice
1 1/2 oz. bourbon

Set aside a large, attractive sprig of mint that has been washed, lightly blotted, and dipped in powdered sugar. (Kudos to Goodwin.)

Fill a whiskey sour or Collins glass with crushed ice.

In a mixing glass or cup, muddle remaining sprigs of mint, water, and granulated sugar, then (leaving crushed mint behind) pour over ice, followed by bourbon. Stir. Garnish with sugared mint sprig and serve with straw.

Frozen Julep

This recipe is the author's adaptation, a combination of two recipes, one from Sennet and one from Poister.

---

6 mint leaves

1 oz. sugar syrup

1 oz. lemon juice

2 oz. bourbon

6 oz. crushed ice

mint sprig (for garnish)

Muddle mint leaves with syrup, lemon juice, and bourbon in a bar glass. Place in a blender with the crushed ice and mix for 15 to 20 seconds at high speed (or until the ice becomes mushy). Pour into a pre-chilled double Old Fashioned glass, garnishing with the mint sprig.

Punchbowl Julep

This adaptation from Sennett is suitable for parties.

---

4 doz. mint sprigs
4 oz. powdered sugar
8 oz. (1 cup) cold water
2 bottles bourbon

Fill a large punch bowl with ice and scrunch a smaller one inside. In this, muddle three dozen mint sprigs, sugar, and water, then fill with crushed ice and pour bourbon over it. Garnish the mixture with remaining, broken, mint sprigs. To serve, ladle up mixture, catching some mint each time, and pour into tall glass.

Diet Julep

For the diet conscious, the following recipe—which eliminates the sugar and lowers the alcohol content—will please.

---

5 sprigs fresh mint
$^1/_2$ packet aspartame sweetener
1 oz. water
crushed ice
$1^1/_2$ oz. bourbon

Muddle 4 sprigs of mint, sweetener, and water in bottom of julep cup or glass, fill with crushed ice, followed by bourbon. Stir and garnish with remaining sprig of mint.

JULEP VARIATIONS

—⦁⦁⦁—

In their *The World's Best Bartenders'
Guide*, Scott and Bain state that
"the Mint Julep is synonymous with
bourbon," but they acknowledge
that "there have been those who've
created their own versions of this
fabled drink." For example, there is a
concoction that substitutes for the
bourbon an ounce each of brandy and
peach-flavored brandy and that is called
a "Georgia Mint Julep." Some
other variations follow.

Essence of Julep

It is not always possible to obtain fresh mint (or for bars to stock it). As a contingency, one can substitute mint oil or extract (oil in alcohol), but be sure to read the label: Some mint extracts consist of, or include, peppermint, which should be avoided. Try Wagner's Spearmint Extract[36] or LorAnn Gourmet Spearmint Oil.[37]

---

spearmint oil or extract
1 tsp. sugar
$1/2$ tsp. water
crushed ice
2 oz. bourbon

In a julep cup or glass mix sugar with water and a drop of spearmint oil or 5 or so drops of extract. (You will need to experiment to determine the exact amount.) Stir until sugar is dissolved, then fill cup with crushed ice, add bourbon, and stir.

Mint Cordial (1839)

Although not strictly a julep recipe, this old "receipt" for a cordial (a sweetened spirit or liqueur) is certainly, well, julepesque. Its ingredients—fresh mint, whiskey, sugar, and (to dilute for serving) water—show its kinship with the historical Kentucky drink. Here is the entry in the words of Mrs. Lettice Bryan from her book *The Kentucky Housewife.*

Mrs. Bryan also gives "receipts" for quince, grape, gooseberry, and other cordials, noting: "The principal design of these cordials is to preserve the juice, to use when the fresh materials cannot be procured, as it is much cheaper than to use the essence, and the flavor is equally as nice." She notes that "rectified whiskey" is that concentrated by redistillation.

Gather some young tender stalks of mint early in the morning; pick off the leaves, put them in a jar, pour on enough rectified whiskey to cover them, close the jar, and set it by for two days. Then squeeze out the mint, and fill up the jar again with fresh mint. Repeat this the third and fourth time; lastly, strain it, add two pounds of sugar to each gallon of the brandy, and bottle and cork it up for use. When you wish to make use of it, dilute it to the proper strength with water, and add more sugar.

Julep "Receipt" (1900)

The following is taken from the *Kentucky Receipt Book* (1900), reportedly from "the copy used by Louisville's prominent Seelbach family early this century."[38]

One quart of water, 2 cups sugar, 1 pint of claret wine, 1 cup of strawberry juice, 1 cup orange juice, juice of 8 lemons, 12 sprigs of fresh mint. Make a syrup of boiling water and sugar. Break mint in pieces and add to boiling water. Cover and let it stand 5 minutes, strain and add to syrup. Add fruit juice. Pour in punch bowl and add claret and cracked ice. Dilute with water. Add fresh mint and whole strawberries.

Honey Mint Juleps

This recipe is adapted from one that appeared in *Southern Living* magazine.[39]

---

1 cup water
1 1/2 cups fresh mint
1 cup honey
crushed ice
3 1/2 cups (28 oz.) bourbon
mint sprigs

Bring water to a boil in a small saucepan and remove from heat. Add the mint, stirring until it is wilted, then add honey, stirring until it is dissolved. Allow mixture to cool and strain to remove mint.

To make a mint julep, combine 2 oz. bourbon with 2 tablespoons of the honey mint syrup and pour over ice in a frosted glass or julep cup. Stir. Garnish with the sprigs of mint.

Serves 14.

Champagne Julep

This recipe is another julep variant, adapted from *The Bartender's Bible*.[40] Champagne is substituted for water in this elegant variation.

---

6 mint leaves
1 tsp. superfine sugar
2 oz. bourbon
4 oz. champagne

In a bartender's mixing glass, place four mint leaves, sugar, and several drops of water. Muddle thoroughly and add bourbon, stirring well. Strain the mixture into a Collins glass, adding ice cubes and Champagne. Garnish with the two remaining mint leaves.

Gin Julep

As we have seen, juleps can be made not only with bourbon but also with other liquors. Following is a recipe for a gin version.

mint syrup (see "Kentucky Derby Mint Julep")
2 oz. gin
fresh mint sprigs

In a julep cup or old-fashioned glass, mix 2 oz. gin and mint syrup to taste. Fill with ice and garnish with mint sprig.

NON-ALCOHOLIC JULEPS

For anyone wishing an alternative
to the traditional julep, here are some
non-alcohol versions that are tasty drinks
in their own right.

Mint Julep Tea

A delicious iced tea results from substituting tea for bourbon in a standard mint julep recipe.

---

mint syrup (see "Kentucky Derby Mint Julep")
iced tea
crushed ice
mint sprig

Combine iced tea and mint syrup (to taste) over crushed ice in an iced-tea glass. Stir. Garnish with mint sprig.

Apple Mint Juleps

For those wishing a non-alcoholic julep this fruit-juice version from Gunter should fill the bill.

---

2 cups fresh mint, chopped
8 cups apple juice
$1/2$ cup fresh-squeezed lime juice
mint sprigs (for garnish)

In a large saucepan, combine the mint with the apple juice and bring to a boil. Remove from heat, cover, cool, then chill thoroughly in refrigerator.

Using a wire-mesh strainer, pour the mixture into a $2^{1/2}$-quart pitcher and stir in the lime juice. Serve over shaved or crushed ice and garnish with mint sprigs.

Serves 8.

YOUR OWN MINT JULEP RECIPE

———⁌∞⁍———

After suitable experimenting and
arriving at your own philosophy of
mint-julep making and deriving your own
formula, you may set it down here with
your signature and date.

My Own Mint Julep

_____

_____

_____

_____

_____

_____

_____

_____

_____

_____

_____

_____

SIGNATURE

_____

DATE

The Bourbon Trail

SHANNON LAMKIN

THE BOURBON TRAIL

The Kentucky Bourbon Trail is a charming tour of seven of the country's oldest bourbon distilleries. The Trail offers a look at the art and science of bourbon production set among the treasures of Kentucky's landscape: babbling streams, rolling hills, and picturesque thoroughbred farms. And with the seven distilleries within 35 to 40 miles of one another, a tour that includes all of them can be completed in one or two days.

Bourbon is a signature aspect of Kentucky's rich history. Widely regarded as the crown jewel of the distilling industry, Kentucky currently produces nearly 95 percent of the world's supply of bourbon. No other state can boast the combination of natural resources that give bourbon its distinctive flavor and characteristics. Corn grown on Bluegrass farms is combined with Kentucky's calcium-rich, iron-free limestone water to produce the mash. The oaks of the region are used to make the virgin barrels that hold the aging bourbon, and the region's cold winters and hot summers allow the whiskey to expand and contract against the charred wood of the barrel, producing the unique taste and aroma of America's only native spirit. Be-

The Filson Historical Society.

cause of these distinctions, Kentucky is the only state allowed to put its name on a bottle of bourbon.

All seven distilleries on the Bourbon Trail follow the same basic steps for producing Kentucky's "liquid gold," but variations in their recipes and production process make each brand distinctive. Each distillery tour is also a special event.

Maker's Mark
3350 Burks Spring Road
Loretto, Kentucky
(270) 865-2099

Nestled among the streams and hills of Happy Hollow is the Maker's Mark distillery. With its unique red shutters and wood-framed buildings, it is one of the most aesthetically pleasing stops on the Bourbon Trail. In addition to its bourbon legacy, the site boasts a collection of beautifully restored historic structures such as the Original Owner's House and the Quart House, which is believed to be America's oldest retail package store. But the primary motivation of most visitors is to witness the process that produces one of the world's most esteemed bourbons. Established in 1805, Maker's Mark is the nation's oldest working distillery still located on its original site, and it is also one of the smallest. Maker's Mark takes great pride in its distilling process, including the fact that they use only pure limestone water from neighboring Hardin's Creek. They produce their bourbon by hand in small quantities to ensure its superior flavor. After visitors learn how this Kentucky classic is produced, they are invited to hand-dip their own bottle of Maker's Mark to create its signature red wax seal.

Wild Turkey
U.S. Highway 62 East
Lawrenceburg, Kentucky
(502) 839-4544

The Wild Turkey distillery sits atop Wild Turkey Hill overlooking the Kentucky River near Lawrenceburg. Bourbon has been produced on the site since 1893, but it wasn't until some fifty years ago that the product found its name, after businessman Thomas McCarthy Sr. offered his now-famous spirit to his friends on a turkey shoot. Wild Turkey prides itself on using simple, old-fashioned methods to produce its bourbon. In keeping with that philosophy, the appearance of the distillery is plain and austere. Visitors can see where the grain arrives for inspection and watch it being transferred into the massive fermentation vats. They can also visit the timbered warehouses where this special bourbon ages and takes on its distinctive flavor.

Labrot and Graham
7855 McCracken Pike
Versailles, Kentucky
(859) 879-1939

A visit to the historic Labrot and Graham distillery in Versailles is a special experience. The oldest, smallest, and slowest working of all the distilleries on the Bourbon Trail, it sits among the scenic horse farms of central Kentucky. The nearly two-hundred-year-old limestone buildings still stand on the site and have been restored as a means of celebrating the old methods of bourbon making. Labrot and Graham is the only Kentucky distillery that still uses copper pot stills, the traditional technique used in whiskey distillation. While most bourbon is aged for at least four years, the master distiller at Labrot and Graham feels that each barrel has a different maturation rate and uses strict standards of color and aroma to determine when a barrel is ready to be bottled (usually 5 to 7 years). Tourists can enjoy a specially prepared picnic on the porch of the visitor's center from spring through fall.

Heaven Hill
1064 Loretto Road
Bardstown, Kentucky
(502) 348-3921

Heaven Hill distillery in Bardstown is America's largest independent, family owned producer of distilled spirits. It was founded by the Shapira brothers in 1935, shortly after the repeal of Prohibition. An informative tour of the grounds includes a look at the rows of open-rick warehouses that hold the second largest supply of aging bourbon in the world. Visitors will learn about Heaven Hill's special filtering procedure and the secret of the master distiller's age-old sour mash process. They can also witness how the aged bourbon barrels are opened and emptied under the careful scrutiny of the distiller. Heaven Hill's best selling bourbon is named after Kentucky's first commercial distiller, Evan Williams. The distillery still uses the same recipe that Williams perfected over two hundred years ago.

Buffalo Trace
1001 Wilkinson Boulevard
Franklin County, Kentucky
(502) 696-5926

Named after the ancient buffalo crossing that was once on the site, Buffalo Trace distillery sits on the banks of the Kentucky River near Frankfort, Kentucky. A working distillery has been located on the site since 1787; Buffalo Trace was one of only four distilleries in the United States that was allowed to produce single-barrel bourbon, which is whiskey drawn from one lovingly aged and carefully observed barrel. A tour of the distillery includes an intriguing look at the historic holding warehouses where the bottled bourbon is aged under careful temperature specifications.

Four Roses
1224 Bonds Mill Road
Lawrenceburg, Kentucky
(502) 839-3436

The Four Roses distillery offers a glimpse at an uncommon bourbon-making method. The site was built in the early 1900s to resemble the architecture of southern California, featuring classic Hacienda-style Spanish construction. Though internationally acclaimed, Four Roses bourbon is less well known in the United States than some of its counterparts, largely because its straight bourbon whiskey could not be purchased in this country until 1998. Tours begin at the massive grain silo that stores only the most carefully selected corn, rye, and barley. The master distiller at Four Roses uses an unconventional method of bourbon production, using no less than ten different recipes and mixing the results to produce the line of rich, smooth, mellow spirit for which the distillery is famous.

Guided tours are available by appointment only.

Jim Beam
149 Happy Hollow Road
Clermont, Kentucky
(502) 543-9877

A visit to the Jim Beam American Outpost in Clermont presents a revealing look at the history of bourbon making as well as the compelling story of the Beam family, who have practiced the art of distilling for over two hundred years. The Jim Beam brand is available in more than 120 countries and is the world's top-selling bourbon. It is estimated that each year more than 2.2 billion individual drinks of Jim Bean bourbon are consumed. The distillery boasts a series of exhibits that demonstrate the science of bourbon making from start to finish. The American Outpost also features historical treasures such as the T. Jeremiah Beam home, which has been lovingly renovated to its original 1911 style and is listed in the National Registry of Historic Places. The grounds also house an authentic moonshine still, believed to be the oldest in America.

NOTES

1. Poister, *New American Bartender's Guide.*

2. Godbey, "Mint Julep."

3. Quoted Carson, *Social History,* 214.

4. Regan, *Bartender's Bible.*

5. Quoted "Mint Julep."

6. Carson, *Social History.*

7. Simmons, *Illustrated Herbal Handbook,* 68-71; Hoffman, *Book of Herb Cookery,* 172.

8. www.botanical.com

9. Markey, *Kentucky Jug.*

10. "Mint Julep."

11. Seranne, *Southern Junior League Cookbook,* 593-94.

12. Regan, *Bartender's Bible,* 32-33.

13. www.thebucknerhome.com

14. *Encyclopedia Britannica,* s.v. "whiskey."

15. Poister, *New American Bartender's Guide.*

16. Crowgey, *Kentucky Bourbon,* 124-43.

17. Ibid.

18. *American Drinks,* History Channel.

19. Sennett, *Complete World Bartender Guide*; Poister, *New American Bartender's Guide.*

20. Poister, *New American Bartender's Guide*.

21. Carson, *Social History*, 215.

22. Candace Perry, quoted "Mint Julep."

23. Quoted "Mint Julep."

24. Quoted Carson, *Social History*, 214.

25. www.thebucknerhome.com

26. Markey, *Kentucky Jug*.

27. Quoted Baker, "Controversy."

28. Baker, "Controversy"; Ferguson to author.

29. Cotton, *Old Mr. Boston*, 65.

30. Baker, "Controversy."

31. Hoffman, *Book of Herb Cookery*, 172.

32. Sennett, *Complete World Bartender Guide*.

33. Regan, *Bartender's Bible*, 33.

34. www.kentuckyderby.com.

35. "Old Bardstown Mint Julep."

36. Wagner's, Ivyland, PA 18974.

37. www.lorannoil.com

38. "Derby Time!"

39. "Honey Mint Juleps."

40. Regan, *Bartender's Bible*.

REFERENCES

American Drinks: History in a Glass. 2001. Television documentary, History Channel.

Baker, Bonni. 1976. "Controversy: No One Agrees on Julep Recipe!" *Lexington Leader* (Lexington, Ky.), April 29.

Bryan, Mrs. Lettice. 1839. *The Kentucky Housewife.* Reprinted Paducah, Kentucky: Collector Books, n.d.

Buckner, Simon Bolivar. 1909. Quoted in http://www.thebucknerhome.com/julep/history.html

Carson, Gerald. 1963. *The Social History of Bourbon.* New York: Dodd, Mead.

Cotton, Leo, ed. 1935. *Old Mr. Boston De Luxe Official Bartender's Guide.* 23rd printing. Boston: Mr. Boston Distillery.

Crowgey, Henry G. 1971. *Kentucky Bourbon: The Early Years of Whiskeymaking.* Lexington, Ky.: The University Press of Kentucky.

"Derby Time!" 2001. www.oldlouisville.com/Derby/Default.htm

Ferguson, Jay. 2000. Personal communication from director of curatorial services, Kentucky Derby Museum, Louisville, Ky., September 3.

Godbey, Marty. 1992. "Mint Julep." In Kleber, *Kentucky Encyclopedia,* 641.

Goodwin, R. Eriks. 2001. "The Virginian Mint Julep Recipe." http:/
/www.unimatrix.com/eriks/favorites/mintjulep.html

Gunter, Julie Fisher. 1999. *The Ultimate Southern Living ® Cookbook.* Birmingham, Ala.: Oxmoore House.

Hoffmann, Irene Botsford. 1940. *The Book of Herb Cookery.* Boston:
Houghton Mifflin.

"Honey Mint Juleps." 2001. http://globalgourmet.com.

Johnson, Samuel. 1755. *A Dictionary of the English Language....*
Reprinted New York: Barnes & Noble, 1994.

Kentucky Derby, 128th. 2002. "Mint Julep." www.
Kentuckyderby.com.

Kleber, John E., ed. 1992. *The Kentucky Encyclopedia.* Lexington,
Ky.: The University Press of Kentucky.

Markey, Gene. n.d. [1967.] *The Kentucky Jug.* Lexington, Ky.: The
Kentucky *Jug Society.*

"Mint Julep." 2001. http://hotwired.lycos.com/cocktail/97/17/
nc_drink.o.week.html

Nickell, Joe. 1990. *Pen, Ink & Evidence: A Study of Writing and Writing Materials for the Penman, Collector, and Document Detective.*
Reprinted New Castle, Delaware: Oak Knoll Press, 2000.

———. 2000. "Historical Sketches: Mint Julep," *Licking Valley Cou-
rier*, April 27.

"Old Bardstown Mint Julep." N.d. *Spring & Summer Selections* (bro-
chure). Bardstown, Ky.: The Willett Distilling Co. (from their publication, *Cooking with Bourbon*).

Perry, Candace. 2001. Cited in "Mint Julep."

Poister, John J. 1999. *The New American Bartender's Guide.* New York: Signet.

Regan, Gary. 1993. *The Bartender's Bible.* New York: HarperPaperbacks.

Scott, Joseph, and Donald Bain. 1998. *The World's Best Bartenders' Guide.* New York: HPBooks.

Sennett, Bob, ed. 1993. *Complete World Bartender Guide.* New York: Bantam Books.

Seranne, Ann, ed. 1977. *The Southern Junior League Cookbook.* New York: David McKay.

Simmons, Adelma Grenier. 1972. *The Illustrated Herbal Handbook.* New York: Hawthorn Books.

Smith, J. Soule. 1949. *The Mint Julep: The Very Dream of Drinks.* Lexington, Ky.: The Gravesend Press. Recipe reprinted in *Kentucky Alumnus*, Spring 2000, 26.

ACKNOWLEDGMENTS

I am grateful to Ken Cherry, former director of the University Press of Kentucky, and Angelique Cain Galskis, managing editor, for encouraging creation of this book. Angelique also heads the list of those who assisted in collecting recipes and other information. Others include Timothy Binga (director, Center for Inquiry Libraries), Jay R. Ferguson (Kentucky Derby Museum), Lucille N. Haney (my beloved aunt), Frank O'Neill, Carol Reimondo, Petar Siljegovich, and the staff of the Department of Special Collections at the University of Kentucky's Margaret I. King Library. Shannon Lamkin researched and wrote the section on Kentucky's Bourbon Trail, and she and Gena Henry located the photos that enhance the text. I am also grateful to Ranjit Sandhu for manuscript assistance.

THE BOURBON TRAIL

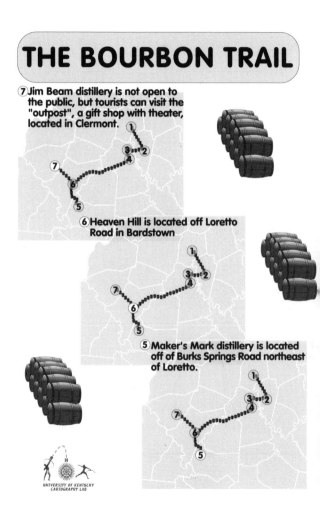

7. Jim Beam distillery is not open to the public, but tourists can visit the "outpost", a gift shop with theater, located in Clermont.

6. Heaven Hill is located off Loretto Road in Bardstown

5. Maker's Mark distillery is located off of Burks Springs Road northeast of Loretto.

UNIVERSITY OF KENTUCKY
CARTOGRAPHY LAB